FULL MOON IS RISING

BASHO

Full moon is rising.
Around, forever around:
my dreams . . . revolving.

FULL MOON IS RISING

"Lost Haiku" of Matsuo Basho
(1644-1694)

and

Travel Haiku of Matsuo Basho:
A New Rendering

By

JAMES DAVID ANDREWS

Boston
BRANDEN PRESS
Publishers

ACKNOWLEDGMENTS

I thank Nobuyuki Yuasa and Penguin Books Ltd. for permission to quote in my Preface and in the Appendix several selected prose passages and verse from *Basho: The Narrow Road to the Deep North and Other Travel Sketches*, trans. Nobuyuki Yuasa (Penguin Classics, 1966), pp. 84, 57, 58, 77, 129, 137 f., 63, 79 f., 83, 59, 110, 92, 68, 133, 52, 55, 60, 76, 128, 138, and 71 f. Copyright © Nobuyuki Yuasa, 1966; reprinted by permission of Penguin Books Ltd.

My pen-and-ink drawings for the main illustrations in this book are original but quite imperfect modifications of ancient Japanese art, as follows: the frontispiece picture of Basho is adapted from a portrait in the Itsuo Museum, Ikeda City, Osaka; the picture facing Section I is adapted from *Pink and White Plumblossoms*, by Ogata Korin (1658-1716); the picture facing Section II is adapted from *Winter Landscape*, by Sesshu (1420-1506); the picture facing Section III is adapted from *Waterfall*, by Shingei (1431-1485); and the picture facing the Appendix is adapted from a series of *Flowers-and-Birds* by Kano Motonobu (1476-1559). The latter four pictures can be found in such collections of Japanese art as *Pageant of Japanese Art*, Volume 2: *Painting: 14th-19th Centuries*, ed. Masao Ishizawa *et al.* (Tokyo: Toto Shuppan Co.; and Rutland, Vermont and Tokyo: Charles E. Tuttle, Co., 1957).

The incidental designs are adapted from Japanese family crests of the sixteenth and seventeenth centuries as depicted by Kosaku Ito in *Early Japan*, by Jonathan Leonard (New York: Time-Life Books, Time, Inc. 1968). The jacket illustration is adapted from a photograph in *Junichi: A Boy of Japan*, by G. Warren Schloat, Jr. (New York: Alfred A. Knopf, 1964) which was provided originally for that book by the Consulate General of Japan in New York.

To
MATSUO BASHO
who created beauty amid suffering

and

NOBUYUKI YUASA
who recaptured beauty in translation

CONTENTS

PREFACE

The immortal haiku of Matsuo Basho (1644-1694) sparkle forever fresh. Among haiku lovers, Basho's group of travel sketches with haiku is rightly regarded as a masterwork.

In addition to offering now a new rendering of his travel haiku, I believe you will want to know in what way the present book includes "lost haiku" of Basho.

They are not "lost haiku" in the sense that I, or others, have just discovered a crumbling seventeenth-century manuscript on which these haiku, previously unknown, were inscribed in the original Japanese.

No. These are "lost haiku" by being poems that (in some instances) Basho might well have chosen to write, but did not. Let me explain.

The material in the superb book, *Bashō: The Narrow Road to the Deep North and Other Travel Sketches*, as translated from the Japanese by Nobuyuki Yuasa (Penguin Classics, Penguin Books, 1966), was written by Basho as a prose narrative with haiku interspersed.

The Yuasa translation includes about 200 haiku written by Basho (mainly) and his travel companions, plus a few quoted poems by earlier authors whom Basho admired.

Reading that book in English, I was also impressed by the poetic vividness of many of Basho's prose narrative sections. And I asked myself what would happen if some of the *prose* jewels in Basho's narrative were transformed into haiku — especially in those places where Basho *could* have given us a haiku but did not. This book is partly in answer to that question.

What I have done is, first, to provide a new rendering of each of the haiku that Basho did write in his travel sketches. It happens that in his 1966 translation, for reasons given in his Introduction, Mr. Yuasa did not put Basho's travel haiku into the classic seventeen-syllable (5-7-5) form. Instead, he used a four-line form of varying quantity. In my new rendering here, the 5-7-5 form is used throughout. So far as I know, this complete group of Basho's travel haiku has never, until now, appeared in English in the 5-7-5 form. In the Appendix to this volume, I give further reasons for doing the new rendering.

My second effort was to try to recreate some of the "lost haiku." As a result, I have now sprinkled in among Basho's own haiku some eighty-four new haiku that Basho might have written but did not. *The interspersed "lost haiku" are italicized to set them apart from Basho's haiku,* newly rendered. I hope you will like the combination. The page numbers in my Preface and text and Appendix refer to the Yuasa translation for easy reference.

A previous book of my haiku, entitled *Five-Seven-Five*, was published in 1974 by The Golden Quill Press, Francestown, New Hampshire. Mr. Yuasa himself, now in Hiroshima, has been most kind in referring to that book as a "beautiful achievement." The usefulness of the present work, however, should be judged apart from my earlier book.

If this is sufficient explanation, you may prefer to go now directly to the haiku. If you desire more about why it seemed especially appropriate to try to recapture some of the "lost haiku," you may find these further thoughts as fascinating as I did.

(1) Despite the fact that Basho was a seasoned artist, he was occasionally so overwhelmed by the beauty he was experiencing, or by recalling what some previous master had written at that same place, that he made no attempt at poetry on that occasion. For example, he writes:

During my three days' stay in Yoshino, I had a chance to see the cherry blossoms at different hours of the day — at early dawn, late in the evening, or past midnight when the dying moon was in the sky. Overwhelmed by the scenes, however, I was not able to compose a single poem. (p. 84)

Elsewhere, Basho has this comment:

Hiring a boat at the port of Yoshizaki on the border of the province of Echizen, I went to see the famous pine of Shiogoshi. The entire beauty of this place, I thought, was best expressed in the following poem by Saigyo.

> Inviting the wind to carry
> Salt waves of the sea,
> The pine tree of Shiogoshi
> Trickles all night long
> Shiny drops of moonlight.

Should anyone dare to write another poem on this

13

pine tree, it would be like trying to add a sixth finger to his hand. (p. 137 f.)

(2) We must also keep in mind the incredible physical effort and countless hazards involved in Basho's journeys on foot and horseback — storms, cliffs, rapids, mountains, highwaymen, night wanderings, disease, and all the rest. Among diseases, his particular "complaint" was dysentery, a chronic companion that finally felled him — on October 12, 1694 — at age fifty.

These physical strains and hazards often made it impossible for Basho to write haiku at a particular time and place, as is indicated in such passages as this:

I had a bath in a hot spring before I took shelter at an inn. It was a filthy place with rough straw mats spread out on an earth floor. They had to prepare my bed by the dim light of the fire, for there was not even a lamp in the whole house. A storm came upon us towards midnight, and between the noise of thunder and leaking rain and the raids of mosquitoes and fleas, I could not get a wink of sleep. Furthermore, an attack of my old complaint made me so ill that I left the inn upon the first hint of light in the morning. I suffered severely from repeated attacks while I rode on horseback bound for the town of Kori. It was indeed a terrible thing to be so ill on the road, when there still remained thousands of miles before me, but thinking that if I were to die on my way to the extreme north it would only be the fulfilment of providence, I trod the earth as firmly as possible . . . (p. 110)

(3) There is humor as well as irony in recalling another problem Basho faced — that of mere interruption. Thus:

When dusk came, we sought a night's lodging in a humble house. After lighting a lamp, I took out my pen and ink, and closed my eyes, trying to remember the sights I had seen and the poems I had composed during that day. When the priest saw me tapping my head and bending over a small piece of paper, he must have thought I was suffering from the weariness of travelling, for he began to give me an account of his youthful pilgrimage, parables from ṣacred *sutras,* and the stories of the miracles he had witnessed. Alas, I was not able to compose a single poem because of this interruption. (p. 92).

(4) In his travel sketches, Basho is most conscientious in crediting his companions with any haiku that they, not he, wrote on the journeys. Basho not only gives them due credit, but he is also generous in encouraging others to join him in artistic creation.

For all these reasons, I believe Basho himself would look with beneficence on this effort to bring to birth some of the "lost haiku" that stir in embryo within his prose narrative.

Attempting this, I have in some cases kept some of Basho's own individual words as rendered by his translator, Mr. Yuasa. In most instances I have used new phrasing, so as to compress considerable portions of prose into the creative confines of a

15

haiku's slender framework. In each case the result is not a quotation, but rather is distinctly a new haiku.

All of the prose passages quoted above are taken from the Penguin Classics paperback edition already cited. Mr. Yuasa's book has also an excellent Introduction that illustrates the gradual development of the haiku form, and gives the interesting story of Basho's life.

The 1966 Yuasa translation comprises five of Basho's travel sketches with haiku, a form known as *haibun*. To provide a break only where Basho began a major new journey, I have arranged the haiku in three sections, but have noted where the other two begin.

Regarding haiku #2 and #6, readers may recall that Basho's adopted city of Edo became, some centuries later, the great metropolis of Tokyo.

For readers who are interested in writing haiku, or in some of the principles of translating haiku from other languages into English, the brief examples in the Appendix to the present book may be useful.

I thank Nobuyuki Yuasa and Penguin Books for their permission to quote the passages given above and some haiku in the Appendix; Gladys Young for introducing me to the Yuasa translation; and my wife, Ruth Elliott Andrews, for helpful comments during preparation of the manuscript. I also appreciate the inspiration of many who are currently writing excellent haiku, such as: Foster Jewell and Rhoda Jewell, Michael McClintock, Evelyn Tooley Hunt (Tao-Li), Robert Spiess, Willene H. Nusbaum, Nick Virgilio, Emily Romano, Gustave Keyser, Mary Dragonetti, Lorraine Harr, and Geraldine C. Little. Many of these, and other poets of similar ability, have not only written major books, but also contribute to such haiku magazines as *Bonsai, Byways, Dragonfly, Janus-SCTH, Modern Haiku, Seer Ox, Tweed,* and others.

In a future edition, I plan to enhance the "line unity" of some of my renderings here. Whatever the imperfections in my work, my desire has been to convey more fully to English readers Basho's deep humanity, engaging humor, passion for beauty, courageous endurance, and (in the phrase of Michael McClintock) his "quiet brilliance."

The frontispiece haiku was inspired by a fragment of verse that Basho is said to have spoken to one of his disciples, Donshu, as Basho lay dying (see Yuasa, Introduction, p. 47 f.).

Completing that haiku, I have tried to recapture across the centuries the spirit of Basho, and to imagine what the haiku could have been if Basho had lived to finish it. The key to the present solution finally came when, after struggling with the question, I took a walk by moonlight and then recalled Basho's poetic statement that ". . . all who have achieved real excellence in any art, possess one thing in common, that is, a mind to obey nature, to be one with nature, throughout the four seasons of the year. Whatever such a mind sees is a flower, and whatever such a mind dreams of is the moon." (Yuasa, p. 71 f.) Earlier, I had rendered that in 5-7-5 form:

> Oneness with nature:
> all objects become flowers,
> all dreams become moon.

With that in mind, it seemed best to complete Basho's deathbed fragment as follows, supplying the missing first line and rearranging the rest:

> Full moon is rising.
> Around, forever around:
>   my dreams . . . revolving.

My closing haiku (preceding the Appendix) was inspired by the prose Postscript that was added to Basho's manuscript by his friend and scholarly scribe, Soryu (see Yuasa, p. 143).

> In the far-off sea,
>   mermaids . . . weeping for Basho:
>   their tears become pearls.

Reading Basho's vivid narrative and haiku can be a moving experience, flavored further by his fine sense of humor. And when you have read the present effort, perhaps you will feel, as I do, that you have journeyed side-by-side with that responsive spirit and poetic genius, Matsuo Basho, on his unfailing quest for the unseen that lies in and beyond the irony and beauty of this world.

J. DAVID ANDREWS

Baltimore, Md.
September 4, 1974
(Revised 8/7/75)

PART I

The Records of a Weatherbeaten Skeleton
A Visit to the Kashima Shrine

I intend to fall
    weatherbeaten skeleton:
        wind grieves through my heart.

My home ten autumns:
    my mind turns back to Edo
        as my native town.

(#2, p. 51)

In a way, I'm glad
    not to see great Mount Fuji
        in this foggy rain.

(#3, p. 51)

I left master's home.
    Must entrust its Basho tree
        to Mount Fuji's care.

(#4, p. 52)

Written by Chiri

An ancient poet
    pitied monkeys' cries. But now:
        this abandoned child!

(#5, p. 52)

21

Dear friends in Edo:
do they count days, think of us
at River Ōi?

(#6, p. 53)

Written by Chiri

Roses of Sharon
perish by road, one by one,
in mouth of a horse.

(#7, p. 53)

Horseback, half-asleep:
see far moon, smoke thread rising
for their morning tea.

(#8, p. 53)

Moonless night, pitch-dark:
powerful wind embracing
age-old cedar trees.

(#9, p. 54)

My head clean-shaven,
and dressed like priest, but not one:
dust of world still clings.

(#1-a, p. 54)

Poet Saigyo
would write verse: even woman
cleaning potatoes.

(#10, p. 54)

Butterfly, orchid:
in flame hues of those bright wings
sweet incense burning.

(#11, p. 54)

A spray of ivy,
trained up wall and few bamboos:
invites a tempest.

(#12, p. 55)

Visit my village.
Brothers now wrinkled, hair white:
joy to see alive.

(#2-a, p. 55)

Dead Mother's white hair:
if I touch, my tears will melt
those frail threads of frost.

(#13, p. 55)

23

Sound as sweet as lute:
    plucking of a cotton bow
        from dark bamboo glade.

(#14, p. 55 f.)

How many old priests,
    how many morning-glories,
        died under this pine?

(#15, p. 56)

Yoshino mountains:
    peaks in clouds, vales in white mist,
        ax sounds . . . echoing.

(#3-a, p. 56)

Yoshino valley:
    bell sounds of distant temples
        strike deep in my soul.

(#4-a, p. 56)

Night, utter silence:
    let me hear a fulling-block,
        my good temple wife.

(#16, p. 56 f.)

This world's clinging dust
   I wash off in this pure spring:
      clear droplets of dew.

                                        (#17, p. 57)

At emperor's tomb:
   weedy grass, named "remembrance,"
      recalls bygone days.

                                        (#18, p. 57)

Autumn wind blowing:
   chilling as the icy heart
      Lord Yoshitomo.

                                        (#19, p. 58)

These thickets, fields, all:
   once ruled by proud Fuwa gate.
      The autumn wind blows.

                                        (#20, p. 58)

On my long journey,
   wake from dream . . . am still alive:
      dusk of autumn day.

                                        (#21, p. 58)

Winter peonies,
    and far-off plover singing.
        Cuckoo call in snow?

(#22, p. 58)

Barely an inch long,
    young white fish are shimmering:
        seashore at dawning.

(#23, p. 59)

Shrine of Atsuta,
    walls crumbled, old stones fallen:
        dry "remembrance" weeds.

(#5-a, p. 59)

Ancient shrine ruins:
    weedy memories are dead.
        Eat rice-cake at inn.

(#24, p. 59)

Poetic madness:
    I plod like Chikusai,
        in the wailing wind.

(#25, p. 59)

On a rainy night,
　　I sleep on grassy pillow:
　　　　barking of a dog.

Merchants of the town:
　　I'll gladly sell for profit
　　　　my snow-laden hat.

(#27, p. 60)

This snowy morning,
　　even horse is spectacle:
　　　　must stop to see it.

(#28, p. 60)

Over dark of sea,
　　one speck of soft white, moving:
　　　　voice of flying duck.

(#29, p. 60)

Travelling on road,
　　hat on head, sandals on feet:
　　　　I meet end of year.

(#30, p. 60)

27

In year of the cow:
    cow laden with rice-cake, fern.
      Who is the bridegroom?

(#31, p. 60)

This day in springtime:
    even nameless hills adorned,
      films of morning mist.

(#32, p. 61)

Priests walk hall's cold floor,
    water-drawing observance:
      sound of wooden clogs.

(#33, p. 61)

Cover of white plum:
    where are cranes, stolen or hid
      behind plum blossoms?

(#34, p. 61)

Within plum orchard,
    sturdy oak takes no notice
      of flowering blooms.

(#35, p. 61)

Day of reunion:
    shed your glad tears on my sleeves,
        Fushimi peach blooms.

(#36, p. 61)

Along my hard way
    on mountain road, greeted by
        violet smiling.

(#37, p. 62)

Lighter than blossoms
    of cherry, like far mirage:
        Karasaki pine.

(#38, p. 62)

Wild azalea branch
    in pail. Woman is tearing
        meat of dried codfish.

(#39, p. 62)

Patch of yellow rape:
    wild sparrows, now pretend to
        admire the flowers.

(#40, p. 62)

On our reunion,
    cherry-tree blooms between us:
        our lives now made one.

(#41, p. 62)

Together let us
    share these simple ears of wheat,
        grass pillow tonight.

(#42, p. 63)

Weeping, pay homage
    the lovely white deutzia.
        Plum blossoms . . . scattered.

(#43, p. 63)

Butterfly, poppy:
    he would tear off his own wings
        as a gift of love.

(#44, p. 63)

Having suckled deep,
    bee creeps out from hairy depths
        of sweet peony.

(#45, p. 63)

A traveling horse:
    what luxury to eat wheat
        at a friendly inn!

(#46, p. 64)

Though lacking much else,
    on road my summer robes gained:
        gathering of lice.

(#47, p. 65)

Crouched all night by pine,
    I watch full moon, and ponder
        Chunagon's sorrow.

(#48, p. 65)*

Quoted poem by Teishitsu

*Robe black as a crow,
    priest with long staff strides off, first:
        free pass Nirvana?*

(#6-a, p. 65)

*Not priest or plain man,
    I waver always, like bat:
        not quite bird or mouse.*

(#7-a, p. 65)

Rising from grass plains,
like two swords piercing the sky:
Mount Tsukuba's peaks.

(#8-a, p. 66)

Snow beauty, and more,
as Mount Tsukuba shines forth
in those purple robes.

(#49, p. 66)

Herds of wild horses
prancing proudly on the grass.
And wild stags, belling.

(#9-a, p. 66 f.)

View of the full moon
blocked by rain, I fret. Find peace
at priest's hermitage.

(#10-a, p. 67)

The moon glows the same:
it is the drifting cloud forms
make it seem to change.

(#50, p. 68)

Written by the priest

Moon moving swiftly
    across sky. Treetops below
      are dripping with rain.

(#51, p. 68)

Written by Tosei*

I slept in temple,
    and so with a solemn look
      I now watch the moon.

(#52, p. 68)

Written by Tosei

Bamboo slept in rain.
    Now it is standing upright
      for viewing the moon.

(#53, p. 68)

Written by Soha

Within the temple,
    how lonely to view the moon:
      patter of eavesdrops.

(#54, p. 68)

Written by Soha

Venerable pine:
    in day of the ancient gods,
      the merest seedling.

(#55, p. 68)

Written by Tosei

Solemn penitence:
let us wipe dew-drops gathered
upon temple stone.

(#56, p. 69)

Written by Soha

Raising mournful cries,
even stags kneel down, worship
before sacred shrine.

(#57, p. 69)

Written by Sora

In half-reaped paddies,
a lone crane. In the village,
autumn deepening.

(#58, p. 69)

Written by Tosei

Beneath this bright moon
over village, let me help
farmers harvest rice.

(#59, p. 69)

Written by Soha

A farmer's young child,
while hulling rice, stops his hands
to gaze at the moon.

(#60, p. 69)

Written by Tosei

On burnt-over ground,
    potato leaves. Wait, tiptoe:
      rising of the moon.

(#61, p. 69)

Written by Tosei

My trousers will dye
    bright hue, among bush-clovers
      now in fullest bloom.

(#62, p. 70)

Written by Sora

Middle of autumn:
    horses graze till full, lie down
      in flowering grass.

(#63, p. 70)

Written by Sora

Bush-clovers, be kind:
    bed this pack of mountain dogs,
      at least for the night.

(#64, p. 70)

Written by Tosei

My dear sparrow friends:
    sleep, please you, haystack-enclosed
      at my humble house.

(#65, p. 70)*

Written by host, Jijun

Your house standing here,
    cedar-foliage enclosed,
        pregnant with autumn.

(#66, p. 70)*

Written by guest, Basho

Our calls halt a boat
    coming up river: we start
        our moon-viewing trip.

(#67, p. 70)

Written by Sora

PART II

The Records of a Travelworn Satchel
A Visit to Sarashina Village

In my bony frame:
  wind-swept spirit, thin as veil,
    stirring to write verse.

(#11-a, p. 71)

Oneness with nature:
  all objects become flowers,
    all dreams become moon.

(#12-a, p. 71 f.)

From this day forward
  I shall be called wanderer:
    embark in showers.

(#68, p. 72)

You will again sleep,
  night by night, nestled among
    camellia blooms.

(#69, p. 72)*

Written by Chotaro

Winter now . . . spring comes:
  your bundle will contain blooms,
    Yoshino cherry.

(#70, p. 72)

Written by Rosen

39

Before my journey,
*   friends gave me gifts and parties:*
*   great man goes forth? Ha!*

(#13-a, p. 73)

Diary, be vivid!
*   tiny hut . . . lost in mountains,*
*   lonely inn on moor.*

(#14-a, p. 73)

Plovers' sounds call me,
    near "Starlit Promontory":
        stare into darkness.

(#71, p. 74)

Beach of Narumi:
    vast sea separates me from
        ancient capital.

(#72, p. 74)*

I am just halfway
    to the ancient capital.
        Clouds laden with snow.

(#73, p. 74)

40

Cold night is about:
   but we feel safe together,
      sleeping in same room.

(#74, p. 74)

Sunlight of winter:
   upon horseback, on cold ground
      my stiff shadow froze.

(#75, p. 75)

Pebbles on the beach,
   the white stones of Irago:
      I will stop for go.

(#15-a, p. 75)

Heights of Irago:
   my singular luck to see
      a lone hawk, circling.

(#76, p. 75)

The Atsuta Shrine:
   on flawless glassy surface,
      pure flowers of snow.

(#77, p. 75)

41

Pass of Hakone
    on this cold snow-filled morning:
        surely someone goes.

(#78, p. 76)

Smoothing the wrinkles
    of my coat, I start walk to
        snow-viewing party.

(#79, p. 76)

Viewing snow landscape,
    let me walk far as I can
        till I stumble, fall.

(#80, p. 76)

Early plum fragrance:
    searching, I find it by eaves,
        this stately storehouse.

(#81, p. 76)

Idle day at inn,
    at year's end, I see people
        dusting their houses.

(#82, p. 76 f.)

42

Like half-starved poet
  Sogi: I climb steep slope to
    Brace-self-on-stick Pass.

(#16-a, p. 77)

Crossing this high pass
  on foot, with stick, would spare me
    this fall from my horse.

(#83, p. 77)

At end of the year,
  weep to arrive, at last, home:
    umbilical cord.

(#84, p. 77)

At least, second day
  of year I will rise early,
    welcome floral spring.

(#85, p. 77)

Freshness of springtime,
  world is only nine days old:
    these fields, these mountains!

(#86, p. 78)

Springtime, heated air:
  tiny waves, of inch or two,
    above wintry grass.

(#87, p. 78)

Old temple ruins:
  Buddha statue moss-covered,
    except shining face.

(#17-a, p. 78)

From stone foundation,
  heated air shimmers up to
    the crumbling statue.

(#88, p. 78)

In garden, I stand
  staring . . . cherry tree. My mind
    sees things of the past.

(#89, p. 79)

Flooded with sweet scents,
  I stand now before this tree:
    do not know its name.

(#90, p. 79)

In this stormy wind
     of February, a bit
          cold to be unclothed.

(#91, p. 79)

Speak of loneliness:
     deserted mountain, old man
          digs wild potatoes.

(#92, p. 79)

Pointing to young leaves,
     rush plant: "I must know the name,"
          I said to scholar.

(#93, p. 79)

A young shoot, bearing
     beautiful flowers, now grows
          on this old plum tree.

(#94, p. 79 f.)

In potato fields,
     old gate stands half-buried in
          fresh leaves of goose grass.

(#95, p. 80)

For sacred virgins,
    how befitting: this lone stock
        of most fragrant plum.

(#96, p. 80)

What good luck I have:
    see picture of Nirvana,
        this sacred compound.

(#97, p. 80)

I must travel on!
    cherry trees of Yoshino
        now bloom in my mind.

(#18-a, p. 80)

We write on our hats:
    "Vast universe, no fixed home,
        we two wanderers."

(#19-a, p. 81)

Be patient a while,
    you'll see Yoshino cherries
        my dear cypress hat.

(#98, p. 81)

Be patient a while,
    my fond hat: you too will see
        Yoshino cherries.

(#99, p. 81)

Written by companion, Mangiku-maru

Pack load on my back:
    coats, note paper, food basket.
        Knees and steps falter.

(#20-a, p. 81)

I tire of walking:
    inn is snugly embraced by
        wisteria blooms.

(#100, p. 81)

This night in springtime:
    man in corner of temple,
        sits meditating.

(#101, p. 82)

Walking in high clogs,
    priests going in rain that falls
        on blooms of cherry.

(#102, p. 82)

Written by Mangiku

47

Lord of this mountain,
 be kind to show me your face
  in dawning blossoms.

(#103, p. 82)

At summit of pass
 I climb into air, take breath,
  high above the lark.

(#104, p. 82)

A spray of blossoms
 on Dragon's-Gate waterfall:
  good gift for tipplers.

(#105, p. 82)

Tipplers, be joyous
 to learn of this blossom bridge
  across waterfall.

(#106, p. 83)

Yellow rose petals
 drop one-by-one in silence:
  roar of waterfall.

(#107, p. 83)

I walk five, six miles
   every day, looking for you:
      blossoms of cherry.

(#108, p. 83)

Against storm-dark sky,
   cherry blossoms, and sad plant
      called "bloom tomorrow."

(#109, p. 83)

My fan for a cup,
   under scattering cherry
      I pretend to drink.

(#110, p. 83)

The rains of springtime
   must have filtered through the leaves
      to make crystal spring.

(#111, p. 84)

Clouds of cherry blooms,
   dawn, evening, deep night: beauty
      overwhelms my pen.

(#21-a, p. 84)

Mountain pheasant calls.
   I yearn with warmest love for
      my father, mother.

                                   (#112, p. 84)

At most sacred shrine:
   my head hair, humbled under
      scattering cherry.

                                   (#113, p. 84)

Written by Mangiku

Reach this southward bay,
   Wakanoura: at last
      meet fleeting springtime.

                                   (#114, p. 84)

Wandering the world,
   simple food, empty-handed:
      no fear of robbers.

                                   (#22-a, p. 85)

On way, I find some
   who love art: genius . . . in weeds,
      gold . . . buried in clay.

                                   (#23-a, p. 85)

For lighter feeling
    I take off a kimono,
        put it in back-pack.

(#115, p. 86)

Moment I descend
    Mount Yoshino, I'll sell my
        cotton-padded coat.

Written by Mangiku

(#116, p. 86)

Is it divine thought
    that this tender fawn is born
        day of Buddha's birth?

(#117, p. 86)

Statue of blind one,
    let me wipe your eyes' salt tears
        with these fresh soft leaves.

(#118, p. 86)

Just as stag's antlers
    are split in tines, so I go,
        apart from my friend.

(#119, p. 87)

Wandering journey:
    pleasant, our casual talk
        of iris flower.

                    (#120, p. 87)

Summer at Suma.
    Moon in sky, but scene empty:
        someone is absent.

                    (#121, p. 87)

I do see the moon,
    but I am not satisfied;
        summer at Suma.

                    (#122, p. 87)

Mountains dark with trees;
    dawn light on Ueno hills
        reddens the ripe wheat.

                    (#24-a, p. 87 f.)

At sunrise I see
    fishers' tanned faces amid
        white poppy flowers.

                    (#123, p. 88)

Small fish, spread on sand:
to keep crows off, villagers
with bows and arrows.

(#25-a, p. 88)

Mount Tetsukai:
slipping, clinging, we climb path
to gateway of clouds.

(#26-a, p. 88 f.)

Off from the sharp point
of a fisherman's arrow:
cry of wild cuckoo.

(#124, p. 89)

Where cuckoo's voice glides
down the sky and meets the sea,
I find an island.

(#125, p. 89)

Temple of Suma,
shade of a tree. Thought I heard
ancient flute on march.

(#126, p. 89)

Confined in trap-pots,
    octopus may still rejoice:
        night . . . and summer moon.

(#127, p. 89)

Had I reached this beach
in autumn's vast loneliness:
    greater poems? Ha!

(#27-a, p. 89)

Province of Tamba.
    Ridge road leads on to sheer cliffs:
        "Hell's Gate," "Headlong Fall."

(#28-a, p. 90)

From this precipice:
    ancient battle scene . . . and sea's
        melancholy roar.

(#29-a, p. 90)

Autumn wind blowing:
    soon I must see full moon rise,
        Mount Obasute!

(#30-a, p. 91)*

In distant past: place
old women were left to die
among lonely rocks.

(#31-a, p. 91)

We climb mountain road
steep with peril. Make missteps,
we laugh to keep brave.

(#32-a, p. 91)

Weary priest on way —
grim, bent, and breathless with load;
we carry his pack.

(#33-a, p. 91)

Perched on horseback load,
cliff drops thousand-feet . . . river:
please, horse, do not jerk!

(#34-a, p. 91 f.)

Local guide, on horse,
dozes serenely. My fear:
headlong over cliff.

(#35-a, p. 92)

Moonlight drifts through leaves,
*   and chinks in wall, to my floor:*
*   autumn loneliness.*

(#36-a, p. 92 f.)

Small country village,
*   innkeeper brings us gross cups:*
*   we drink by moonlight.*

(#37-a, p. 93)

Rural sky, big moon:
*   feel like decorating it*
*   with gold-lacquer art.*

(#128, p. 93)

Over precipice,
    ivy vine clinging to bridge:
        body and soul, joined.

(#129, p. 93)

Way to Kyoto:
    imperial horses crossed
        high suspended bridge.

(#130, p. 93)

On suspension bridge:
 when fog lifted, I dared not
  even wink my eye.

(#131, p. 93)

Written by Etsujin

Imagined: sitting
 with old woman, both in tears,
  gazing at the moon.

(#132, p. 94)

Moon, sixteen days old:
 still I linger in village
  of Sarashina.

(#133, p. 94)

Three days have gone by:
 three times I have seen bright moon
  ride the cloudless sky.

(#134, p. 94)

Written by Etsujin

With its slender stalk,
 yellow valerian stands
  bedecked in dewdrops.

(#135, p. 94)

Hot radish piercing
　　my tongue, while the autumn wind
　　　　is piercing my heart.

From Kiso mountains,
　　horse-chestnuts will be my gifts
　　　　to city-people.

Now bidden goodbye
　　and bidding farewell, I walk,
　　　　autumn of Kiso.

Four different gates,
　　four different sects: as one
　　　　beneath the bright moon.

Suddenly a storm
　　comes down on Mount Asama,
　　　　blows grit over me.

PART III

The Narrow Road to the Deep North

Lured by roving wind,
  like ancients who died on road:
    I must wander on.

(#38-a, p. 97)

My mind is possessed:
  dreams of moon over far isles.
    Sell my house . . . and go.

(#39-a, p. 97)

High grass at my door.
  New generation will come:
    Festival of Dolls.

(#141, p. 98)

Behind me . . . my friends;
  before . . . three thousand hard miles:
    tears blinding my eyes.

(#40-a, p. 98)

Birds are now mourning,
  and fish weep with tearful eyes:
    passing of springtime.

(#142, p. 98)

Ashore, my friends stand
in a row, wave faithfully
till I disappear.

(#41-a, p. 99)

I climb Mount Nikko,
feel shrine's most sacred power:
bright beams of sunlight.

(#42-a, p. 100)

At the sacred shrine:
with awe I see fresh green leaves
shining in sunglow.

(#143, p. 100)

My head shaved of hair,
we reach Mount Kurokami,
don clean summer clothes.

(#144, p. 100 f.)

Written by Sora

Summer observance:
silently, from inside cave,
I watch waterfall.

(#145, p. 101)

Daybreak, lonely moor,
   farmer lends me his own mount:
      "This horse knows the way."

(#43-a, p. 102)

Dear small girl, your name
   Kasane means "manifold":
      double-flowered pink.

(#146, p. 102)

Written by Sora

Reaching a village,
   I send back the farmer's horse:
      money on saddle.

(#44-a, p. 103)

In summer mountains
   I bow at feet of statue,
      ask journey blessings.

(#147, p. 103)

I would gladly leave
   my small grassy hermitage —
      except . . . it's raining.

(#148, p. 104)

Quoted poem by priest, Buccho

Tiny hermitage
in summer grove: woodpeckers
have left it unmarked.

(#149, p. 104)

Turn your horse's head
sideways, to field, so I may
hear cry of cuckoo.

(#150, p. 105)

Wrapped in noxious gas,
where dead insects cover ground,
stands the Murder Stone.

(#45-a, p. 105)

Girls planted one square,
paddy-field. I rise from rest,
shade of willow tree.

(#151, p. 105)

Beyond the great gate:
rising wind, fields of white blooms,
like first autumn snow.

(#46-a, p. 106)

In humble clothing,
      pass great gate: adorn my hair,
            white deutzia blooms.

(#152, p. 106)

Written by Sora

At "Reflection Pond,"
      where all is mirrored cleanly:
            today . . . just grey sky.

(#47-a, p. 106)

Beyond the great gate,
      rice-planting songs of far north
            bring forth first poem.

(#153, p. 107)

Chestnut tree by eaves,
      in splendid bloom: unnoticed
            by those of this world.

(#154, p. 108)

I search hill country
      from pond to pond: hope to find
            katsumi iris!

(#48 1-1a, p. 108)

The rice-planting girls:
   their busy hands remind me,
      old dyeing method.

(#155, p. 108)

Husbands killed at war,
   two young wives donned their armor:
      I weep at their graves.

(#49-a, p. 109)

With flying banners
   show proudly, sword and satchel:
      May Festival Day.

(#156, p. 109)

Bed at dirty inn,
   midnight storm, leaking roof, fleas:
      I slept not a wink.

(#50-a, p. 110)

Early wet season.
   To Kasajima, how far?
      Endless muddy road.

(#157, p. 111)

Be sure my master
    sees pine of Takekuma,
        far-north cherry blooms.

(#158, p. 111)

Written by Kyohaku

Saw cherry blossoms
    and, three months later, marvel:
        twin trunks of the pine.

(#159, p. 111)

Today, May the Fourth:
    throw leaves of iris on roof
        and pray for good health.

(#51-a, p. 111 f.)

Hills of Tamada:
    white rhododendron blossoms;
        and bush-clover . . . soon.

(#52-a, p. 112)

Kinoshita woods:
    dense dark pines, dew falls like rain.
        Bring an umbrella.

(#53-a, 112)

Gift of straw sandals
with laces dyed a deep blue:
iris flowers bloom.

(#160, p. 112)

Taga castle site.
Mossy shaft, thousand years old.
Tears are in my eyes.

(#54-a, p. 113)

Masshozan temple.
Among trees, scattered tombstones:
sad . . . we all must go.

(#55-a, p. 114)

Darkening May sky,
island stark in clear moonlight:
fishermen's voices.

(#56-a, p. 114)

Late on moonlit night,
blind minstrel sings to his lute,
songs of distant past.

(#57-a, p. 114)

Matsushima isles,
scattered in cupped seaside bay:
ocean tides, rising.

(#58-a, p. 115)

Matsushima bay.
Isles above and joined to isles:
parent, child . . . caress.

(#59-a, p. 115 f.)

Ojima Island,
small huts: I yearn to go in.
Moon rises on sea.

(#60-a, p. 116)

Alone in my room.
Moon, wind, swift clouds are haunting:
Matsushima isles.

(#61-a, p. 116 f.)

Oh, clear-voiced cuckoo:
to span Matsushima isles,
need crane's silver wings.

(#161, p. 116)

In a spacious bay,
Kinkazan isle, and old mine:
"Flower-blooms of gold."

(#62-a, p. 117)

Brief summer grasses:
of ancient warriors' dreams,
only this remains!

(#162, p. 118)

I catch a far glimpse,
Kanefusa's hoary hair:
white deutzia blooms.

(#163, p. 119)

Written by Sora

The long rains of May
left untouched this Gold Chapel,
aglow in deep shade.

(#164, p. 119)

Bitten by fleas, lice.
Near my pillow I hear sound:
horse urinating.

(#165, p. 120)

Guest . . . house with fresh air:
 I sleep with lazy comfort,
  as if I owned it.

(#166, p. 121)

Silkworm nursery.
 Crawl out bravely, show your face:
  voice of a lone toad.

(#167, p. 122)

Holding powder-brush
 within my view, I now stroll
  among the rouge-plants.

(#168, p. 122)

Silkworm nursery:
 men and women, splendid dress,
  like the ancient gods.

(#169, p. 122)

Written by Sora

Sacred temple site:
 on all-fours from rock to rock,
  I bow at each shrine.

(#63-a, p. 122)

From silent temple,
  voice of a lone cicada
    penetrates rock walls.

(#170, p. 123)

Linked verse, once cast here,
  took root, bore flowers each year:
    clear note of reedpipe.

(#64-a, p. 123)

River Mogami,
  small boat, steep mountains each side:
    Silver-Threads Cascade!

(#65-a, p. 123)

Gathering May rains,
  River Mogami speeds down:
    one turbulent stream.

(#171, p. 124)

Truly blessed is this
  South Valley: gentle wind breathes
    faint snow-aroma.

(#172, p. 124)

Sacred shrines of north:
    beams of moon, lamps in darkness,
      illumine the world.

(#66-a, p. 125)

Climb up Mount Gassan,
    gateway of clouds to sun, moon:
      I spread leaves and sleep.

(#67-a, p. 125)

Gassan the swordsmith
    tempered his fine swords, this stream:
      crystal-clear waters!

(#68-a, p. 125 f.)

Three-foot cherry tree,
    for six months in mountain snows,
      bravely blooms in June.

(#69-a, p. 126)

Pale new-moon shining
    over dark Mount Haguro:
      feel how cool the night.

(#173, p. 126)

Over Mount Gassan:
　　how many cloud forms rise, melt,
　　　　before moon comes up?

(#174, p. 126 f.)

Forbidden to tell
　　secrets of Yudono shrines,
　　　　tears flood on my sleeves.

(#175, p. 127)

As I step on coins
　　on sacred Yudono road,
　　　　tears rush to my eyes.

(#176, p. 127)

Written by Sora

I enjoy cool breeze,
　　Fuku-ura beach. Behind:
　　　　Mount Atsumi . . . sun.

(#177, p. 127 f.)

River Mogami:
　　into its surging waters,
　　　　flaming sun . . . drowning.

(#178, p. 128)

Wind rises from sea,
*   am half-blinded by sand, rain:*
*   must dream of beauty.*

(#70-a, p. 128)

Cherry by lagoon:
*   I sail over blossom waves,*
*   as Saigyo said.*

(#71-a, p. 128)

Vast view of lagoon:
*   Mount Chokai supports sky*
*   like a great pillar.*

(#72-a, p. 129)

A blooming silk tree,
    Kisagata rain: sad tears,
        Lady Seishi.

(#179, p. 129)

Shiogoshi beach:
    cranes are dabbling their long legs
        in cool flow of sea.

(#180,. p. 129)

This festival day,
    Kisagata: what special
        delicacy here?

(#181, p. 129 f.)

Written by Sora

Sitting with full ease
    at doors of huts, fishermen
        enjoy cool evening.

(#182, p. 130)

Written by Teiji

What sacred instinct
    taught these birds? No waves so high
        as to flood their homes.

(#183, p. 130)

Written by Sora

*Hundred miles and more
    my goal, as storm clouds gather:
        I force myself on.*

(#73-a, p. 130)

Night sky now looks changed,
    sixth of July: tomorrow,
        Weaver meets lover.

(#184, p. 130)

The grand Milky Way,
in one arch spans wave-capped sea,
then falls to Sado.

(#185, p. 131)

Drifting on, nightly,
like white froth on ocean shore:
two young prostitutes.

(#74-a, p. 131)

Under same inn roof,
all slept: prostitutes and I.
Bush-clovers and moon.

(#186, p. 132)

Famed wisteria
of Tako, past wild mountains:
I'll never see them.

(#75-a, p. 132)

I walked among clouds
of ripening rice. Below:
Angry-Sea waters.

(#187, p. 133)

My friend's silent grave,
    move, if you hear my speaking.
        My wails . . . autumn wind.

(#188, p. 133)

This cool autumn day.
    Simple dinner: peel by hand,
        cucumbers, eggplant.

(#189, p. 133)

Red, red glows the sun,
    ignoring season. Wind knows:
        early chill, coming.

(#190, p. 133)

Dwarfed Pine: gentle name.
    And gently the wind stirs through
        bush-clovers, pampas.

(#191, p. 134)

Lord Sanemori's
    helmet: two curved horns, dragon,
        gold chrysanthemums.

(#76-a, p. 134)

Famous old helmet:
   amazing, from dark recess,
   a cricket singing.

(#192, p. 134)

Enroute to hot spring:
   white peak of Mount Shirane
   overlooks my back.

(#77-a, p. 134)

The shrine of Kannon,
   fine rocks, old pines in garden:
   goddess of mercy.

(#78-a, p. 134 f.)

It is far whiter
   than white rocks of Rock Temple:
   autumn wind, blowing.

(#193, p. 135)

Yamanaka spring:
   bathed in ease, I have no need
   chrysanthemums' health.

(#194, p. 135)

Wherever on road
    I fall, bury me nearby:
        blooming bush-clovers

(#195, p. 136)

Written by Sora

Alas, from now forth,
    dewdrops, erase my hat words:
        "A party of two."

(#196, p. 136)

All night long I hear,
    behind temple: autumn wind
        moaning on the hill.

(#197, p. 136)

Written by Sora

Sora, companion,
    fell ill. Yesterday he left:
        seems a thousand miles!

(#79-a, p. 135, 137)

Last night, howling wind.
    At daybreak, the chanting priests.
        Now, the breakfast gong.

(#80-a, p. 137)

Repay host's kindness:
  I would gather willow leaves
    scattered in garden.

(#198, p. 137)

Shiogoshi pine:
  trickles with drops of moonlight,
    as Saigyo said.

(#81-a, p. 138)*

Goodbye, my old fan:
  scribbled it, so now discard.
    The end of summer.

(#199, p. 138)

Cottage of poet:
  moon-blooms, gourds, cocks-comb, goosefoot:
    but he is not home.

(#82-a, p. 139)

Near an old castle,
  above hill called Homecoming:
    cry of early geese.

(#83-a, p. 140)

Before shrine altar,
*   silent moon shines on white sand:*
*   sheen of autumn frost.*

(#84-a, p. 140)

Bishop Yugyo first
    brought sand, on which the bright moon
        shines divinely pure.

(#200, p. 140)

I travel far north:
    changeable skies block my views
        of full autumn moon.

(#201, p. 141)

Lonelier to me
    than Suma beach: autumn ends
        on this twilit sea.

(#202, p. 141)

Mixed with tiny shells,
    scattered bush-clover petals
        roll with the sea waves.

(#203, p. 141)

My journey ended,
*   friends rejoice in my return,*
*   as if from the dead.*

(#85-a, p. 142)

Tightly glued clam-shells
    fall apart, autumn: and I
        must walk on. Farewell . . .

(#204, p. 142)

POSTSCRIPT

In the far-off sea,
    mermaids . . . weeping for Basho:
      their tears become pearls.

APPENDIX

EXAMPLES OF THE TECHNIQUE OF WRITING AND TRANSLATING HAIKU FROM OTHER LANGUAGES INTO ENGLISH

As mentioned in the Preface, my new rendering of Basho's travel haiku is based in part on the excellent translation by Nobuyuki Yuasa of *Bashō: The Narrow Road to the Deep North and Other Travel Sketches* (Penguin Classics, Penguin Books, 1966).

In the Introduction to that work (p. 48 f.), Mr. Yuasa gives major reasons for not attempting to use the classic seventeen-syllable, three-line haiku form (5-7-5) for his 1966 English translation.

I believe, however, that the 5-7-5 form for haiku is always feasible and, although not essential, is usually preferable, for reasons given below.

After I completed my new rendering of these Basho haiku, I wrote to Mr. Yuasa, and he graciously replied in a letter dated 2 October 1974, also giving me permission to quote from his translations. He said he is considering doing a revision of his 1966 translation, and that he will see whether he can now "represent the original syllable structure." Thus, it appears that his views on 5-7-5 translation may be changing. He also said, "I have recently finished a translation of Ryokan, in which I have been able to maintain the original 5-7-5-7-7 syllable structure of waka in English."

Thus, the following examples comparing his 1966 translation with my new rendering of Basho's travel haiku are not intended for unflattering comparisons, but rather are given to suggest basic principles that may be of continuing interest to haiku writers and translators.

(1) The sparse and challenging seventeen-syllable haiku form, whether in Japanese or in English, usually requires a terse and telegraphic use of language, as has been well pointed out by such scholars as Harold G. Henderson (see his *An Introduction to Haiku: An Anthology of Poems and Poets from Basho to Shiki,* Doubleday Anchor Books, 1958). With unnecessary words cut out, haiku makes much use of suggestion and subtlety. And with the poetic coupling of comparisons and contrasts that abound in haiku, much of its effectiveness derives from its extreme economy of words. Each haiku is a sketch, a cameo, a vignette; and the reader must exert his own imagination to fill out the picture and re-live the feeling of what is sometimes called a "haiku moment."

Consider these examples, with the 1966 Yuasa translation followed by the new rendering and with both using the printing style of his book. (The haiku numbers and page numbers refer to the Yuasa translation.)

(#18, p. 57)

The weedy grass
Called reminiscence,
Reminiscent of the bygone days
In front of the Mausoleum.

At emperor's tomb:
Weedy grass, named "remembrance,"
Recalls bygone days.

(#19, p. 58)

The autumn wind,
Resembling somewhat
The frozen heart
Of Lord Yoshitomo.

Autumn wind blowing:
Chilling as the icy heart
Lord Yoshitomo.

(#84, p. 77)

Coming home at last
At the end of the year,
I wept to find
My old umbilical cord.

At end of the year
Weep to arrive, at last, home:
Umbilical cord.

(#179, p. 129)

A flowering silk tree
In the sleepy rain of Kisagata
Reminds me of Lady Seishi
In sorrowful lament.

A blooming silk tree,
Kisagata rain: sad tears,
Lady Seishi.

(2) Even within the spare and demanding 5-7-5
form, it is often possible to achieve a smooth and
natural flow of words. Thus:

(#44, p. 63)

Fluttering butterfly
On a white poppy,
He would wrest his wings
For a token of love.

Butterfly, poppy:
He would tear off his own wings
As a gift of love.

(#94, p. 79 f.)

A young shoot has borne
Beautiful flowers,
Growing upon
An aged plum tree.

A young shoot, bearing
Beautiful flowers, now grows
On this old plum tree.

(#107, p. 83)

One after another
In silent succession fall
The flowers of yellow rose—
The roar of tumbling water.

Yellow rose petals
Drop one-by-one in silence:
Roar of waterfall.

(3) Converting terse haiku into a four-line form with no limit on the number of syllables often has the effect of transforming vivid and telling haiku verse into writing that tends toward prose, as perhaps in the following:

(#25, p. 59)

With a bit of madness in me,
Which is poetry,
I plod along like Chikusai
Among the wails of the wind.

Poetic madness:
I plod like Chikusai
In the wailing wind.

(#50, p. 68)

Regardless of weather,
The moon shines the same;
It is the drifting clouds
That make it seem different
On different nights.

The moon glows the same:
It is the drifting cloud forms
Make it seem to change.

(#190, p. 133)

Red, red is the sun,
Heartlessly indifferent to time,
The wind knows, however,
The promise of early chill.

Red, red glows the sun,
Ignoring season. Wind knows:
Early chill, coming.

(4) In my rendering of Basho's travel haiku, I have sometimes included a word or thought from Basho's prose narrative, if it seemed needed to make the meaning of his haiku clear, or to help make the haiku able to stand as an independent creation even if read apart from Basho's narrative. For example, in his narrative related to his haiku #5, Basho states that he had come upon an *abandoned* child, and this fact is important to the effect of the haiku (although Basho did not include it there). Thus:

(#5, p. 52)

The ancient poet
Who pitied monkeys for their cries,
What would he say, if he saw
This child crying in the autumn wind?

An ancient poet
Pitied monkeys' cries. But now:
This abandoned child!

In the narrative related to his haiku #13, Basho tells of visiting his eldest brother, who showed Basho a lock of white hair from their mother, long since dead. If this fact is incorporated into the haiku, it can be read apart from the narrative and yet keep its poignant impact. Thus:

(#13, p. 55)

Should I hold them in my hand,
They will disappear
In the warmth of my tears,
Icy strings of frost.

Dead Mother's white hair:
If I touch, my tears will melt
Those frail threads of frost.

(5) I have usually rendered the Basho haiku in the present tense, believing that this provides more force and immediacy than does the past tense.

Even more important, when possible I have tried to increase the element of suspense (and thus the impact) of the haiku by saving key words, thoughts, or action until the last line. Thus:

(#29, p. 60)

Over the darkened sea,
Only the voice of a flying duck
Is visible—
In soft white.

Over dark of sea,
One speck of soft white, moving:
Voice of flying duck.

(#31, p. 60)

Whose bridegroom may it be?
I see a cow
Loaded with rice-cake and green fern
In the year of the cow.

In year of the cow:
Cow laden with rice-cake, fern:
Who is the bridegroom?

(#80, p. 76)

Deep as the snow is,
Let me go as far as I can
Till I stumble and fall,
Viewing the white landscape.

Viewing snow landscape,
Let me walk far as I can
Till I stumble, fall.

(#178, p. 128)

The River Mogami has drowned
Far and deep
Beneath its surging waves
The flaming sun of summer.

River Mogami:
Into its surging waters,
Flaming sun . . . drowning.

92

One of the major reasons for using the 5-7-5 form when translating from another language into English is that in this way the English reader may best learn fully to know and appreciate haiku. If the English reader is given less terse renderings of haiku, he may never learn to treasure the subtlety and the poignancy of the haiku experience at its best.

Again, I thank Nobuyuki Yuasa for the inspiration of his splendid book, and for joining with Penguin Books in allowing quotation of haiku from the 1966 Yuasa translation, a book that every haiku lover should obtain.

I hope my present effort to render the travel haiku in the classic 5-7-5 form will add to your appreciation of the spirit and genius of the Japanese master, Matsuo Basho.

NOTES

Part I: In the original Japanese and in the Yuasa translation, Basho's verse #65 and #66 were linked-verse in the traditional Japanese style, called *renga*. Here, the host wrote a 5-7-5 haiku and the guest (Basho) responded with a 7-7 couplet. I have rendered each as haiku. This is also the case with Basho's verse #68 and #69, which together formed a 5-7-5-7-7 *waka*.

Basho's verse #72 was attributed by him to Lord Asukai Masaaki. The Yuasa translation renders it in five lines. Verse #73 is the haiku that Basho wrote, with the earlier poem in mind. I have rendered both as haiku.

Haiku #48 marks the beginning of the travel sketch "A Visit to the Kashima Shrine."

With haiku #51, and a few later ones as noted, "Tosei" is another of Basho's own pen names.

Part II: Haiku #30-a marks the beginning of the travel sketch "A Visit to Sarashina Village."

Part III: Haiku #81-a on Shiogoshi pine is based on a poem by Saigyo, which Basho quotes. It is also quoted in full in my Preface.

Entire text: A few of Basho's poems, and some of my "lost haiku," can properly be classed as senryu.